FRENEMY THIEF

THE END OR A BEND?

Written and Illustrated by

Karen Kellock Ph.D.

Manual for Superior Men

This is a complete theory based on Einstein physics,
Political Psychology, Systems Theory
and Archetypal Psychiatry.

FORMULA

All success attraction
All disease obstruction
All recovery elimination

You must fast on all three

OBSTRUCTIONS:

People
Habit
Food

FRENEMY THIEF

Liberal towns are quiet since everyone's afraid to speak. Signs to quit your school: Words like equity, diversity, inclusivity, white privilege, systemic racism. Or cold relationships with those calling you racist. What Trump did for America was phenomenal and to that degree to liberals he's horrible.   The left is protected for everything it does. It's convinced everyone it's not the enemy, but it is.   Tolerance and universal love leads to acceptance of the occult.   Luciferian doctrine: accept *everything* or it's an insult.

BE ALONE AND GET RICH

THEY'RE AFRAID TO BE ALONE
BEING ALONE IS A SUPERPOWER
RESTLESSNESS IS MISERY
RID OF EM, ENVISION THE FUTURE
ENJOY YOUR OWN COMPANY
NO MORE PETTY COMPETITION
PROTECTING YOUR DIVINE FAVOR
THEY ARE BORED AND LONELY
SELFLESS ALTRUISM IS GONE
THE PLIGHT OF YOUNG WOMEN
REFUSE THE DIRTY: BE WORTHY
GET ALONE AND ELEVATE
SAYING YES TO THEIR PROBLEMS
FEELING TIRED AROUND EM
PEACE OF MIND: THE NEW RICH
SOLITUDE MAKES YOU RICH
NO DOING WHAT THEY'RE DOING

BE ALONE AND GET RICH

THEY'RE AFRAID TO BE ALONE

Those afraid to walk alone will never surpass you. Solitude with God is key to your pursuits.

They have too many distractions and blessing blockers around, tho' they tout the line full-blown.

When God gives an opportunity of a lifetime, He isolates you. Those who can't take it fall behind Sue.

Those who make friends easily tolerate more until they blindly accept things in order to be popular.

When alone God pours out so many blessings you can't receive em but it takes great strength friend.

The friendship thing and people-pleasing left me feeling jaded: compromised, dulled & disappointed.

At one point I just withdrew. My husband and I just wanted to be together alone and we grew.

BEING ALONE IS A SUPERPOWER

Being alone is a super power. It puts you ten steps ahead of everyone behind you like ex-lovers.

Every time you go back to past people you lose: you lose time, insights, money and energy too.

Most of all you lose your train of thought. You can't even think straight around em like you ought.

BE ALONE AND GET RICH

Most cannot sit alone for more than thirty minutes. The promise never arrives to these dimwits.

Chosens: you cannot be around people all the time and get to the next level, giving entry to the devil.

You become your own worst enemy by hanging out with the enemy: i.e. time wasters blocking destiny.

RESTLESSNESS IS MISERY

Your own misery is caused by restlessness. You can't sit still, you always seek out others: it's useless.

You always gotta be around friends. When will you make time for yourself? THEN you'll get well.

My past was hellish cuz I was around the wrong people at the wrong time: always in reaction, aye.

All you need for total success is just to ENJOY your own company. I love being alone & always am see.

When rid of em you do things YOU love to do: they've been shelved for years around those two.

RID OF EM, ENVISION THE FUTURE

When rid of em I could envision the future all day long without them hanging around, what fun!

I finally realized that when alone I got my joy back, my peace of mind, my optimistic visions, aye!

From the doldrums I got my strength back, my power back! I now had the heavens, no more lack.

By isolating myself from supposed friends I was trying to fit in with, I shot up to high destiny so rich!

BE ALONE AND GET RICH

Isolation saved my life & destiny. Everyone I knew was faking it: being around em was boring see.

I always had to be around people but then guess what: I was carrying around their spirits, plain nuts.

Then I was having anxiety attacks, seeking out professionals and ending in hospitals.

It was all cuz I was carrying around spirits from OTHER PEOPLE. Being alone was joy, free of evil.

ENJOY YOUR OWN COMPANY

Start enjoying your own company & see how far you can go! Your Father in heaven is rich ya know.

Anxiety attacks and sleepless nights came from them throwing their insecurities on you, aye.

These creepy friends threw shade on my success, hating on me and jealous too, what a mess.

Being alone you're getting ready to take over the world. To free your mind is like a rocket ship girl.

Their demonic spirits jump on you & guess what: you can't sleep or have nightmares cuza those nuts.

The only time you look back is seeing how far you've come--realizing why you deserve a huge sum.

Finally, now you have peace of mind and aren't arguing with anyone. Realize your huge gains son.

NO MORE PETTY COMPETITION

Finally, you're not having to go toe to toe with anyone. Finally, you can just envision your future hon'.

BE ALONE AND GET RICH

Notice how peaceful your life is now, after God removed these people outa your life. Thank Him, aye!

Notice how you have no distractions by yourself. This alone is a huge breath of fresh air as well.

Life is sweet not having energy vampires pulling you down. It's heavenly when it's just you hon'.

PROTECTING YOUR DIVINE FAVOR

Now that they're gone your favor with God is protected. No more ups and downs or feeling rejected.

Every time you went back it's the same argument and debate. You're different but they never changed.

Every time you went back you felt depressed, drained and tired. I remember it well, stuck in the mire.

Throwing shade on your success/dimming your light: that was all you got with those folks, aye.

The mere fact you allowed things to happen showed you had to go thru those hard lessons.

I know what it's like feeling "owned" by people. They won't leave and wanna stay over: it's evil.

I was too weak & they took me over. This alone can wreck your life: I can't forget the unhappy hours.

"You must leave and no you can't stay over": I was too weak to say that, I just wasn't that clever.

THEY ARE BORED AND LONELY

They were bored and lonely and I never was. They wanted to stay so out came their claws.

BE ALONE AND GET RICH

They imposed constantly, wanting a piece of me! I know what it's like before having boundaries.

In my season of treason I felt encroached on my 10,000 people. The feelings were just inconceivable.

The Lord says not to look back but I only feel gratitude that I finally have privacy and sweet solitude.

Don't look back except in gratitude it's over, and how far you've come from being WAY down there.

The social generation destroyed personalities. When eclipsed by another we become ordinary.

You look at them as your "friend" while they only see you as competition. Think about this again.

SELFLESS ALTRUISM IS GONE

Selfless altruism doesn't exist anymore. They want something, that's when they come to your door.

You soon become the company you keep. I would become the worst of the lot from it see.

The contagion of madness: that's how it works in the human herd. The hedge is down, lines are blurred.

You become them until you realize "this is not me". You must RUN into isolation mode and quickly.

The contagion of madness is the core of my work. See it as a flue bug and recognize this curse first.

Never hang with the wrong people who don't push you towards greatness. Be picky or be alone sis.

They were jealous of your favor--divine blessings--and how others loved you: how utterly depressing.

BE ALONE AND GET RICH

They make assumptions of what "love" or "friendship" means then get mad when you don't agree.

You don't wanna be picayune so you let things slide. Soon you've lost all identity and wanna die.

This vital information leads you to the promised land. Your success is seeing people as the problem.

THE PLIGHT OF YOUNG WOMEN

As a young woman I was forever hounded by men. Before my boundaries I felt insane back then.

Don't resent the past when you were weak, you had to go thru all that to learn these lessons see.

When your whole generation thinks socially it's very hard to see the truth of needed individuality.

If I have anything to teach women it's about men. Don't ever give in to what's only good for them.

"Oral sex isn't sex"--are you kidding miss? Get a grip and recognized how you're being used sis.

You're pushed & railroaded into things you have no business doing. Get honor back: you're dying.

Just cuz they expect it doesn't mean you're supposed to do it. Come to a higher plane & worship it.

REFUSE THE DIRTY: BE WORTHY

Refuse doing dirty & they call you unworthy. You don't "love them" like you said: see the truth honey.

Individuality and boundaries is what we came here to learn see--so don't resent the lessons lately.

BE ALONE AND GET RICH

If in sin she won't have strength/boldness to break up or boundary a manipulator so abuse persists.

If in sin she won't have boldness to break up/put boundaries on manipulators so abuse persists.

He hits her then she makes excuses for him after. That is the result of generational manipulators.

True feminism is parents educating boys not to hit girls and girls standing up for self in their world.

GET ALONE AND ELEVATE

When finally alone you start to elevate. You find out you love jazz, taking yourself out to eat or pray.

When alone you come up with certain ideas you'd never cogitate when in the company of idiots.

How can God show you visions around those blessing blockers? It's impossible, not with him/her.

How can you have a vision around imitators and copy catters? Around show offs & mad hatters?

They hate you cuz they ain't you. So now you pick up habits and viewpoints to get approval too.

How to handle bad memories hon': the only time you look back is to see how far you've come.

Every time I looked back it STUNG. Rather than that, think how grateful you are they're gone.

Being alone is a superpower and a gift, since most can't stand being by themselves and feel adrift.

One thing you can't get back is time. Once I figured that out I cut everyone off but my team, aye.

BE ALONE AND GET RICH

Why do you think misery loves company? Cuz they can't be alone: that's the malady of the empty.

The empty need someone to pull down, to be on their level and to be a repository of their insecurity.

Low vibrational entities are energy vampires. Stop running back to old friends or fail forever.

SAYING YES TO THEIR PROBLEMS

When you say "Yes" to them you say yes to their problems. That's how you suffer charlatans.

Look how far you came alone once getting rid of that crowd of empty souls: bright, vibrant gold.

Who needs bantering back and forth, silly comments, officious questions and then all their friends?

People who are nobobies want you a nobody with them. Jealous entities don't want ambitious friends.

Low vibrational energy vampires are LAZY. They need to be revved em up with your wonderful energy.

You are a breath of fresh air, something never seen before. Without you they're stuck on the floor.

FEELING TIRED AROUND EM

When you're with them you feel tired already. They need you but you don't need them, that's it see.

Soon you're miserable and depressed. Counting the minutes til they finally leave, what a mess!

Your absence is their misery. That's the truth but when pulled down you actually need them honey.

BE ALONE AND GET RICH

The minute they leave you feel a burden come off of you. There's nothing like having self back Sue.

Every time I got back home I felt like heaven. It's anointed as God gave me more lessons.

The American dream is based on FREEDOM. You aren't free with losers and wasters hanging around.

All the time wasted, can you imagine if you'd been alone? You'd be a success on your throne.

PEACE OF MIND: THE NEW RICH

Peace of mind is the new rich. You were held back in poverty cuza these spirits around/the witch.

Hanging around entities and their constant problems means you lose, just floundering around.

Time is money from the hunches gained alone vs. the poverty from your empty mind kept so low.

What they call solitary confinement is heaven to the chosen so happy to be with God, alone.

When you finally use your time the right way you become more adamant to keep them away.

When finally alone you have time to come up with new ideas, thoughts and visions: what a trip hon'!

SOLITUDE MAKES YOU RICH

Being alone will make you a multimillionaire. Don't be trapped: FIGHT to be alone, I declare!

The losers are those posting positive pics on Facebook. Things aren't really like that, don't get hooked.

BE ALONE AND GET RICH

If you spend money on pleasures and a nice home believe me losers all wanna come around.

You don't need someone around keeping you safe cuz the angels are there if alone with God, ok?

NO DOING WHAT THEY'RE DOING

You don't need to be doing what they're doing but what you must do to get to the next level, glowin'.

I've been alone for ten years now and have written 98 books, 22 textbooks and done 400+ videos.

God will send you the right friends & mate at the right time. Don't tolerate users in the meantime.

Enjoy life being alone and creative, with a loving God not trapped by false friends and foe relatives.

We all have more evolving to do. Now you can run fast forward and make money you deserve too.

Let those phone calls go to voice mail. Get abundant life back: you need time to think and heal.

Alone, you'll sleep like a baby and deeply. You're rid of other people's spirits & they are really creepy.

The devil is a liar as they project their fears on your faith. Now that shadow's gone and you'll be ok.

Staying out the way and going deep into destiny will be the best decision of your entire life see.

Finding out about people is the pearl of abundant life. Don't fear em, avoid em and you'll be rich, aye.

SOUL THIEF

ENTHRALLED THEN THE DISCARD
GAMED UNTIL FLIP SCRIPT
NEVER ASSUME *ANYTHING*
ONCE YOU SEE IT DENOUNCE IT
VACILLATION INDICATES WEAKNESS
LED CAPTIVE BY LUST
SANCTIFY YOURSELF: SEPARATE
RELEASING A SOUL TIE: BLOCK *WORDS*
BAN ALL HIS WORDS/TRIGGERS
WHEN GAMES START QUEEN'S ARE GONE
WHAT WILL HE FEEL TOMORROW?
A WORM OF A MAN
SOUL TIE DEGRADATION
DOCTRINES OF DEVILS
IF THERE'S SEX, DENOUNCE IT
LOVE THEN APATHY
COME BACK TO SELF/THE LIGHT
SHORTBREAD FASTING
TENACITY OF A BULLDOG

SOUL THIEF

God doesn't want you in this plight so right away you know it's bad: seek rescue now/tonight.

ENTHRALLED THEN THE DISCARD

He was initially enthralled then waylaid by some sympathy project to virtue signal: reject.

Withdraw then consume your own full and complex destiny cuz that oughta keep you busy.

His minimization/discard phase opened you to your glorious higher self today, God be praised.

His final put down: enough to turn you all around and now you're elated cuz it's gold you found.

From now on question everyone and listen to your family and friends. Do you recall what they said?

GAMED UNTIL FLIP SCRIPT

He gamed you until you flipped to a new script and your life opened up to the greats not the twits.

Keep this central: Because it was sexual you had to denounce it to come into a brand new world.

Why she keeps going back: Every time there's a perversion of her principals: how sad.

She say's she's done then comes right back. Her standards are falling each time: fact.

He takes advantage of her weakness and perverts her principals: every time a new perverse low.

SOUL THIEF

Remember in the latter days men would be haters of good--that's you love, so reject this hood!

He comes to mind, you've denounced it and why, he's shut out. That's how it works: no fowls.

You've wasted how many years of life running after this cat? Five, ten--that much waste in fact?

You can humiliate a queen but then she's gone for good see so what have you achieved?

Genius knows leisure is the greatest recharger so never forces workin', the rewards are better.

So he walked you by, he didn't see you for who you are. That's his bloody problem, now go be a star.

VACILLATION INDICATES WEAKNESS

Watch out cuz high vacillation indicates weakness: looking great one day then the next it collapses.

So you had a wondering eye and got caught up with some flashy guy and a massive soul tie.

It was a mental illness and you had it, so what? People get physically ill too then come out of it.

They lose elite friends and potential mates when they switch to jealousy triggers/mind games.

I just want my little shell so all you guys can go back to hell, to save my soul, to save myself.

He sees you as one of many, you're just an option with him. Don't you see the degrading woman?

Children are gullible and trusting but adults should be grownup--that means not assuming ANYTHING.

SOUL THIEF

As you go lower into his hell gradually you're in a place where you don't even recognize yourself.

Teach the youth boundaries or they're up a creek in their teens/twenties surrounded by sickies.

NEVER ASSUME *ANYTHING*

And above all beloved, stop assuming things about any relationship cuz they don't care you twit.

In putting your attention on him for a minute, he could not fulfill the task, he's a sad failure in fact.

He reached his weak spot and relapsed into games and tactics which incur anxiety in the elect.

You're a bad person, not what I want hon', I choose all that God has for me, wisdom/eternal fun.

So you gave your life, love and affections to a clown in a crown. It wasn't the first time you know hon'.

Ok he was using you/you were using him. Now that you know it's not meant to be, sever relations.

God gave His precious/peculiar YOU to Him and he screwed up--that's how you should be thinkin'.

He was your favorite drug but the only problem he was using you/you were using him: a dud.

ONCE YOU SEE IT DENOUNCE IT

Now that you see it's not meant to be you gotta wean yourself off of him and do it immediately.

Once you see the key: it's sexual and denounce the drug you're already free, removing the block.

SOUL THIEF

When you think of him again it'll be a dark foggy vision of him putting you in degrading competition.

Every time she goes back her independence is diminished each/every time she re-engages.

He creeps into houses and takes their independence, leading them away captive like slaves.

LED CAPTIVE BY LUST

He leads her into captivity by her own lusts. He gains control then rips it away/rejects her love.

Many seek a ruler's favor but we're judged by the Lord. Whatcha need a clown in a crown for?

My guests robbed me of my independence and I didn't have a clue. That's the soul tie groove.

We get to a place where their hyper-control brings fear. Walking on eggs, misery for years.

Being fearful makes the victim feel she doesn't know how to live without him now. Clever devil.

Losing your independence makes you fearful and it is automatic because it is biological.

She's so attuned to a creep he becomes a god running her life. Even in apathy he controls the tie.

Tie your life to Delilah and lose everything God put you on earth to do [and she wasn't His plan too].

How to break it: "Come out from among them, touch not the unclean thing and I will receive you".

Separate yourself after seeing what this is all about and you're there, God rescues the repentant.

SOUL THIEF

As he loses control he appears a caricature, a cartoon. You worshipped him but now he's deplumed.

Sanctification: Come out from among them and be ye SEPARATE and now everything's new son.

SANCTIFY YOURSELF: SEPARATE

Sanctify yourself: you have to come out of them to separate. Separation is holy mate.

It'll hurt but not as much as waking up years later realizing you gave your life away to a jerk.

Endure the pain of cutting him outa your life not allowing this cancer to kill you with strife.

I'm just myself, not an age or bemoaning my age. You're the dam ageist always talkin' about it ok?

"Yes" said the saint "there was a lascivious spirit in me too: like you I didn't know what I do".

They think you're bored or lonely and need their company, so they invade to your dismay.

The game is: he tries to break her down. Working against this is hard, it's a serious undertow.

Love: something happens in that one instant and you know everything about the relationship.

RELEASING A SOUL TIE: BLOCK _WORDS_

Since his manipulation is words gotta block access to your ears including anything online sister.

As long as this person has access to speak WORDS into your life he is steering it remotely: strife.

SOUL THIEF

She must realize she's not healthy enough to listen to his words all due to the emotional triggers.

He never deserved an audience but you granted it because you're unhealthy and he knows it.

His written words are equally triggerful so they must be blocked too. One word can make her blue.

BAN ALL HIS WORDS/TRIGGERS

Listening to even one of his words only perpetuates her condition. Postpone all this til later on.

When healthy enough to listen and access his condition she sees he never deserved a conversation.

The danger of words: A person shrewdly uses words to hold her captive and she totally buys it.

In the discard phase he triangulates with others making her feel inferior, a self-worth leaker.

Queens wear the sign: I'm Number One or NO. They're gamed just once and that's it for a bloke.

With her much fair speech she caused him to yield: she **SEDUCED** him with words, like all Jezebels.

She's so unhealthy his words have the capacity to splinter her identity like Humpty Dumpty.

Here he didn't even deserve to have **ONE** word with her but now holds her destiny, a controlling turd.

She caused him to yield by the flattering of her lips, he was robbed by his incapacity to choose it.

Words are the most manipulative and thus dangerous forces on the planet because we buy it.

SOUL THIEF

To heal she must block her ears and eyes but the sick part of her wants to hear from that guy.

Even her constant checking for calls/texts is an addiction making that groove bigger man.

Call on that part desiring to be FREE for that's the opposite to be checking constantly, no way.

WHEN GAMES START QUEEN'S ARE GONE

Queens won't allow addiction to little men or Mr. Big ala Napoleon. When games start she's gone.

Mr. Player was just a demonic roadblock/speedbump to get you to here, a true lady who is superior.

Our ears are gateway to our soul. So we can't give em access to our ears due to a severe undertow.

You can't get your mind right if you keep the wrong stuff in your ears. It's CALCULATED not sincere.

Lust is the engine driving the diabolical bondage she calls love. She needs to block him NOW.

Accept the relationship for what it is--a joke--and stop giving him access to your ears, a yoke.

Your ears & eyes are gateway to your soul yet you let this person's influence take total control?

What you're looking at and listening to is keeping you stuck where you are. Cut it loose, be a star.

The perversions are intentional. The further they move her from what she knows the more control.

Every time she compromises on a sexual standard she loses herself to this individual more.

SOUL THIEF

While she gives him more control over her soul her self-perspective is diminished/she feels old.

Sexual perversion brings such shame that one believes God wants nothing to do with em ok.

WHAT WILL HE FEEL TOMORROW?

That's how he feels right now but will he feel that way tonight or tomorrow? You don't know!

Your most important realization is that its INTENTIONAL. He knows exactly what he's saying girl.

Just when he had her he was compelled to game her and he lost her: that's how the queen learns.

What she tolerates reflects self-love or it's absence and she takes instant note when it deflates.

Suddenly she sees she never needed him and the True Self swings forth, illuminating and brilliant.

Just when he had her he was compelled to make her feel inferior by obvious triangulating with others.

Breaking this massive soul tie would bring a shining new day and extreme lucrative creativity, ole!

A WORM OF A MAN

A worm of a man [mean] will try to break the queen by making her jealous but then she's gone see.

If you game a queen she instantly sees you in a new light. She's gone, you're not her guy.

Renew your self-respect by officially denouncing this relationship. Declare new direction/say it.

SOUL THIEF

She must see the danger of the soul tie, how it's warped her self-worth and blocked her destiny.

Involvement with a narcissist affects biology and psychology. One is drawn in/can't get out easily.

This relationship diminishes her consistently and entirely yet she can't turn away from it see.

SOUL TIE DEGRADATION

A soul tie sexual bond is like quicksand: the more you struggle to get out it pulls you in and down.

Samson went from a king to a slave because he could not denounce a soul tie relationship.

Going back to a bad relationship brings lost consciousness [losing more self in this mess].

We lose self when struggling to be part of the life of another that is not ordained for our life sir.

Struggling to fit someone's life who is not big enough for your future, you lose self cuz it's a diminisher.

She forgets who she is focusing on the other. He breaks her down to her core, controlled by an inferior.

He breaks her down to a place to be managed by an inferior and it's all intentional too dear.

Because she's lost herself she finds identity in an evil association making every day pure hell.

The more she submits to the soul tie the more her spiritual discernment is compromised, aye.

The holy spirit is grieved and shuts down when other influencers come in taking her bound.

SOUL THIEF

She's lost her spiritual discernment and it's even to the point the holy spirit's not saying anything.

She allowed an ungodly man to play God in her life and the result is horror, sadness and strife.

They call the shots, they dictate every move. She gives heed to seducing spirits degrading her too.

DOCTRINES OF DEVILS

As consciences are seared with a hot iron doctrines of devils come thru in lies, hypocrisy and fightin'

In this era doctrines of devils/lies and hypocrisy are very real with demons prominent in what we feel.

The influence of ungodly people influences our spiritual sensitivity and life becomes drudgery/hell.

Burned fingertips with damaged nerves can't feel anymore and that's what happened here.

When she's with someone not ordained for her life/not of God she loses sensitivity/stays flawed.

The sensitivity she has lost is the reason she keeps going back and forth at the highest cost.

Why she goes back: a frustrated support system challenging her decisions has left her in fact.

Past supports must eventually release her to her own choices. Even her parents must acquiesce.

Finally alone: she's become an island now living with the one she needs most to be away from.

People are destroyed for lack of knowledge because they reject it in their network or entourage.

SOUL THIEF

Everyone in her sphere told her about this guy but she rejected it pursuing a sexual soul tie.

God says if you reject knowledge God will reject you so now she's lost her Hedge of Protection too.

Finally the spirit ceases to strive with us. He's DONE and we face the consequences.

If there's a sexual element in a soul tie relationship you've gotta get rid of it. Speak: DENOUNCE it.

Cuz if there's sex even in fantasy that's a soul tie see and the power to kill is there immediately.

IF THERE'S SEX, DENOUNCE IT

If there's sex in it--in any realm sis--you gotta denounce it and get out immediately, RUN don't skip.

To the victim: You must pull back into yourself and say "I don't know this person" and mean it hon'.

All over the world women are controlled thru soul ties and this is common knowledge with guys.

A soul tie is sealed thru the body and the deepest primal urge for sex to proliferate a sick race.

To sex starved Lady: Pull back into not knowing this person who doesn't even deserve a conversation.

Somehow Elmer Fudd wormed his way in to totally control a Ph.D. woman: how disgustin'.

He can either invade you with people or diminish you with his triangulations with the rabble.

One way or another the social generation came thru and you lost YOUR destiny and worldview.

SOUL THIEF

When I think of him now I see multitudes in a row, not the peace and tranquility I now know.

I've got to have peace and tranquility and you provide me sudden anxiety and vacillations see.

I don't wanna train a man how to treat me if he's already too ingrown to even see me.

He thinks he knows it all: fine, he's stopped the information flow and his ego is all he knows.

LOVE THEN APATHY

He's initially captivated then suddenly minimizing and discarding: your cue to EXIT immediately.

It doesn't have to be something you can explain--listen to your inner instincts, what they're saying.

Look for the signpost of narcissism in both male and female: lovebombing then discard to fail.

If you can abandon this fantasy you'll get your happy life back see and be like a child again, free.

See life as a puzzle to figure out and take control. It's an exciting new direction alone and bold.

The minute you see these signposts of a fickle individual return to stability in your private castle.

Sometimes you gotta maintain an unequal yoke. Knowledge saves you here, be distant/well spoke.

Sex thoughts indicate a soul tie to be denounced--to your great relief today or eventually, aye.

With this certitude your grey days turn into glorious happiness even before you leave the mess.

SOUL THIEF

This guy has made you unhappy, never knowing what he'll do next to trigger fears/make you depressed.

Instead of praying he'll come around, pray to denounce this ungodly relationship and do it **NOW**.

For it's the sex bond that gets her into sick cycles of exhilarating highs then hitting bottom.

He feels so superior with you on the begging end but that's gonna end right now my friend.

COME BACK TO SELF/THE LIGHT

For he and his superiority can go to hell, God wants you back in the groove of discovery/success gal.

Just move away and enter the world of billions of others as you never have to see him again, hurray.

If it's not perfect--let alone hurts you constantly--then it's not of God, obviously. Right lady?

Stop conjuring up vain imaginings of him being with you in your world. It's never happening girl.

After denouncing the painful soul tie I could see the moon again, I could feel the sun--oh my!

So that's your key girl: If it's sexual denounce it. You'll be so relieved, you can count on it!

He felt superior to you, he tried to break you down to control you too. Hell with him, now pursue.

He's not your link to success but you thought he was--that's a key to REMOVE yourself for success.

He actually felt superior to you. Let that make you mad cuz he's nothing without his game too.

SOUL THIEF

Tell his gaming spirit to go to hell and withdraw back into your shell with God and the angels.

Let his foolish spirit misconstrue the information and do himself in--for he'll soon be a has-been.

I'd rather be in hell then play his gambling cards making me feel devastated every single day.

Write out a therapeutic play of all the tactics he's using and you'll see a broad picture of controlling.

Instead of crying in a self-esteem leak, transcend this INTENTIONAL system by truly SEEING it.

If it's sexual and you're sad, it's a soul tie/bad. See the system, know why it's happening, facts.

It's taking sex--a primal urge--to break down and control, first. Don't let it: lasciviousness is a curse.

HEALTHY CANDY/COOKIE BREAKFASTS
SHORTBREAD FASTING

Why I like healthy candy breakfasts: It's most calories in least mass. Even fruit bloats this lass.

What do we need: glucose for energy and animal fat for satiety, the skin and the brain see.

Sugar, flour and butter fills the bill and makes excellent breakfast meals: the shortbread fast is real.

Shortbread fasting and military rations. Who thought of it: Karen Kellock, a proud Scotchwoman.

Even melon later makes me burp burp burp. Only nothing works and there is no hunger sir.

God says fast and tell no one. They'll always try to talk you out of it--eat your shortbread, done.

SOUL THIEF

Food is over-rated, used as entertainment. Superior species are oligophagous: fewest foods.

Think only of your fast not what you hope to accomplish. Leave God to the results and it's magic.

Just think of what you're accomplishing on the fast and everything else will fall into place Lass.

TENACITY OF A BULLDOG

No one has the tenacity of a bulldog like you so no one's been asked to create an empire but you.

Be a lightning rod for the rabble. They need you now cuz they're hamstrung by the anti-bible.

Never force the fit with your work. The true meaning of "patience" is letting it all unfold together.

If heavily conceptual you're invisible before you produce something girl so do it: create for the world.

Handle success like a crate of eggs cuz things can go wrong: what goes up can come down.

One awakens to God then is derailed by boring traditions of men in church: know God first.

There will come a time--YOUR time, a minute--when you'll express your great ideas long muted.

I'm not a preacher or a motivational speaker just a theoretician putting the facts together.

FRENEMY THIEF

Liberal towns are quiet since everyone's afraid to speak, but accepted narratives are ok to preach.

Signs to quit your school: Words like equity, diversity, inclusivity, white privilege, systemic racism.

They're not being educated but indoctrinated.

Contract is the basis of civilization for predictability in all our affairs but not to liberals, I declare.

Left is angry Tommy Robinson got out--the far right neo Nazi or whatever else they call the patriot.

Even smart men are a bit jealous of Trump from intrinsic envy of his SMV (sexual market value).

Academically suspect, ideologically possessed.

It's exhausting/debilitating to be in a cold-hearted relationship with those calling you a racist.

What Trump is doing for America is phenomenal and to that degree to liberals he's horrible.

The left is protected for everything it does. It's convinced everyone it's not the enemy, but it is.

Since self-restraint (saying NO) is a strength that's why weak men get into pornography I think.

Trump has radically expanded scholarships to minorities but the dems can't stand these victories.

Tolerance and universal love leads to acceptance of the occult.

Luciferian doctrine: tolerance, accept everything.

FRENEMY THIEF

2009: 60% of churchgoers voted for liberals. In other words, the baby killing and LGTB agendas.

You can't hate blacks but it's perfectly ok (politically correct) to hate whites.

Tolerance: "Do what thou wilt" is the whole law.

I believe in sin and can see how a church would be popular if it didn't.

They love Bianci's church cuz it won't mention sin just "inclusion"--same old slide into delusion.

Blacks fail from family breakdown/immorality but it's always called racism, that's their reality.

The mob is dumb and vain. Stefan Molyneux

They hate him so much you know he's for real.

Everything is relative, truth is nonexistent, utopia's within our reach: that is what they teach.

Why should utopians be happier than Christians? We have Almighty protecting, they have nothing.

There's nothing like telling truth to democrats and watching them go nuts. Jesse Lee Peterson

In the past, American blacks went to church on Sunday and dad was in the home disciplining.

Al Sharpton and Obama managed to divide the races more than anyone in the history of America.

You don't love your kids sending them to public schools or new scouts intending to destroy good.

FRENEMY THIEF

This is the tyranny of consensus: everyone's afraid to speak in fear of the herd's punishment.

Only good sees evil but evil thinks it's all good can you believe it?

All they're doing by their stupidities is inoculating us against them finally.

Society is obsessed with speaking positively while afraid to speak truthfully = insanity.

They have nothing else but this lie about racism. To keep themselves together it nourishes em.

Such a sad way to live, adapting to the children of the lie--cave into radical agendas then die.

The black experience is hell but from their own behavior not from whites tho' that's what they tell.

When I look at the world it fills me with sorrow. Children today are gonna suffer tomorrow. Jesse

"Racism" is a made up word by race hustlers to keep blacks angry, resentful and controllable.

Even black preachers tout "racism" with the goal to indict whites and get more stuff from them.

The herd is like a flock of birds flying in perfect unison never questioning the flight pattern.

To disarm the people is the best and most effectual way to enslave them. George Mason

FRENEMY THIEF

What Donald Trump is doing for America is phenomenal and to that degree to liberals he's horrible.

No army can stop an idea whose time has come. Victor Hugo

You can't prove things to people so never try to convince them you're not a racist, ever.

Animal farm: Everyone's equal but some are more equal than others.

Mesmerized by his looks and talent I was completely turned off when he opened his mouth.

Getting approval for leftwing activities or liberal viewpoints will make you increasingly outa joint.

So it's Trump's fault they came here illegally and are now being deported split from family?

Labeled our customs, culture/traditions as bigoted, intolerant, repressive and discriminatory.

A sign of a false person/preacher is saying all people are good.

100 year curse: Liberals prove themselves to be meanest most repugnant people on earth.

The herd works off each other's energy like a flock of birds assuming they're on course.

It's culture or sexual licentiousness, can't have both. Culture (like reputation) can vanish like smoke.

FRENEMY THIEF

To veil evil doings they addict us to sex and trash until the moment too late/we don't want that.

They're redundant, take too much time, repeat or get pat, mediocre crummy platitudes/myths.

They hate Trump cuz hating white people is the trend but especially a patriarch worth billions.

Learn from Trump or be blue: Attack back, don't power down, don't worry what they say about you.

They obscure the doctrine of judgement cuz they don't want their sins judged, they love em.

Ever noticed how the most popular are twits?

Correct em and they say "you don't like me" cuz there's no right/wrong: it's called NEWSPEAK.

Trudeau blasting Trump after the deal is made? What poor character this little poser displayed.

Angry mobs have taken over London--sick of treachery like the imprisoning of Tommy Robinson.

Freedom of speech and self-defense are God-given human rights we're losing fast/last chance.

We're forced to self-censure to survive. Countries are falling into complete tyranny, no lie.

"Dignitarian harm" means: I have the right to act as I choose without disparaging remarks.

Censorship is about protecting the monopoly of liberalism and globalism in the public square.

FRENEMY THIEF

Thanks Di Nero for showing us how ugly, unhinged, boorish, and boring Hollywood has become.

Like declining Rome, just when people are most evil we're called to be nice as we virtue signal.

We go from the age of betrayal to the age of straight shooting. Alex Jones

Di Nero must now rely on profane outbursts to be thrust into the public eye since his career died.

Early America was all Christian: helpful but until proof not trusting anyone.

First black president devastated the nation, abused the office and degraded the Whitehouse.

Don't talk to the enemy cuz he'll wear you out with debating insanity, false narratives and realities.

If you wanna make it in Hollywood just say "F--- TRUMP" that's it, cuz they're so intelligent.

They see traces of racism everywhere, they are "tracists". Dennis Miller

Liberal immaturity marked by Newspeak: your correction or criticism means "they don't like me"

Doublethink: All things are true even if in contradiction--a logical fallacy and why you're reactin'.

Ego never questions itself cuz it's Satan (come to steal, kill, destroy) whose actions are reflexive.

The college-brainwashed say it is all wrong but long before you were born we ALL got along.

FRENEMY THIEF

Liberals don't wanna step on anyone's toes except those who know and say so.

They can never see it's a matter of principal. Principals aren't in their lexicon.

Taking life seriously and drawing lines they call being "nerved up".

That's establishing yourself as an artist putting out debauched crap like that? It won't last.

It's either personal attacks or triggering emotions like the current scam over border children.

A coward bows down to the enemy.

Obama the worst president ever don't put up a statue of him we don't ever wanna remember scum.

Lines are drawn/not safe to say anything hon'

An equal playing field means putting up with buffoons.

Dems are so immune to self-corrective critical thought truly they cannot see their absurdities.

Conservatives see good and evil while liberals see race. Jesse Lee Peterson

If you disagree with the racist narrative even with hard facts they'll instantly attack you back.

Nothing more dangerous than a lunatic mob and that's the reason for the second amendment.

FRENEMY THIEF

Plan: Sell house in blue state, move to red state, start brand new life not bringing liberal sin/hate.

You think white racism is bad, black racism is thru the roof. Board up white people/tell the truth.

All angry people feel like victims and reflexively blame someone else for that, it's ridiculous.

Equal playing field tolerates buffoons.

Millions of American prisoners separated from their children and the left has never mentioned them.

Freaking out about non-American children at the border while butchering our own in the womb.

Millennials massively shifting to GOP. They're sick of forced conformity to this leftist crap/unfree.

The news isn't monolithic anymore, it 's channelized. It's two parallel universes, left vs. right.

The SJW mayors of cities and thus the police will take the side of Antifa in the war on the streets.

Walkaway movement has completely taken off. Who knew dumping the Democrats could be cool?

2 classes of people: coastal liberal elites and inland working poor--one is evil, the other we adore.

It's good Californians wanna get the hell out but please don't bring that crap here/we love God.

FRENEMY THIEF

Only after leaving a bad relationship (blue state) for a good one (red) do you realize how bad it was.

Coastal elites are evil that's why you're moving. Tho' liberals are affluent, doesn't mean a thing.

How to walk away: See headless liberal mob attack innocent people in an otherwise happy rally.

I moved to a red state and there were no adjustments save how "real" it all was, escaping scuzz.

We win on the war of ideas, they're so false they must rely on crybabies and bicycle locks.

700,000 homeless American kids and left won't lift a finger to help. Democrats, remove yourself.

Petulant over Hillary's loss they've launched a hate Trump campaign that is lethal and gross.

You can't hide the right. Tho' you don't talk politics to just get along, they know/avoid you on sight.

If you're right, decent, home-loving, patriotic and god-loving they will now hate your guts honey.

Better watch out because the left are petulant children but violent, outa control even the old.

Your art isn't about politics it's about your generation's narrative of such--old slogans outa touch.

In fact when you mimic this crap it's so embarrassing, up the wrong creek/thinking you're chic.

FRENEMY THIEF

A loving mother and strong father is at best unfashionable as the family is being dismantled.

Trump's reversing all of Obama's shrewdly crooked executive orders so be giddy for the future.

Taking on the herd hypnosis that everything goes, you go insane and there's nothing you know.

It's a mentality where virtue signaling reigns supreme cuz no one wants to be out of mainstream.

Having a relationship with media is like dating a woman who twists all you say/no win. Stefan

There's never enough for the left. Stefan Molyneux

The left is a collectivized mind, the right are individualists who don't group protest like dirty slime.

Morning news scene: They know nothing but say the right things, they're part of the team.

What's happened to the left? All they say is vile, disgusting, nauseating even from the best.

Late night comics are the highest paid traitors/brainwashers there are, groomed as big stars.

Late night comics are now just sanctimonious virtue signaling from the anti-Trump resistance.

Trudeau and leftists don't have answers to problems that aren't totally predictable ideologically.

FRENEMY THIEF

It takes a lifetime to develop your own theories otherwise you take on the current narrative/CRAZY.

They don't think, they run an ideology in their head and accept the output without question.

Liberal matrix blocks rational thought which is point by point adaptation to life, the whole lot.

Obama showed a disturbing but crystal-clear pattern of defending black racism towards white folks.

Trump didn't put kids in cages, Obama did that but even so it causes anti-Trump rages.

Why doesn't Joel Osteen discuss the devil, sin or hell? Cuz it's not nice and it sure wouldn't sell

HERETICS: Smiling preachers, yes-men, hell-deniers, globalists, all-is-one nuts/papal communists.

Beta male smiling preachers play both sides and "don't hate anybody" while truth can take a hike.

Wimpy churches don't tell the truth.

There are no "progressive preachers" cuz the Word is ageless applying to all times and spaces.

When people are killed they defend the thugs not the cops. They're calling good evil and evil good.

How can you be a man/woman of God and defend evil? That's what you're doing every day people.

FRENEMY THIEF

Thank you Mr. Trump: a real man after being screwed by a communist who wanted us last in line.

Don't go down that alley into horror/porn, or decades in darkness blocked from life you'd adore.

Horror films are an entry point. These demons are no joke and you'll be irritated, tired, outa joint.

Speak up and be attacked or stay silent and warp your soul. Jordan Peterson

Millennials understood: Dictator killed millions = good. Offensive words = you're a no-good hood.

They don't wanna rip em from their mother's arms but ok to rip em from the womb, that's liberals.

What you're saying is not true though it seems so true cuz you're brainwashed thru and thru.

They weren't just wrong all these years but arrogant in their wrongness (our lives were a mess).

Jesus rebuked the sinner not groveling before him trying to be nice, that's just not so.

If they have perfect knowledge, why does the left fear/hate criticism?

Disputing the liberal stance has been heretical for decades. They'd get mad and we'd concede.

The churches have become wimped to adapt to the wimps in the pew who don't want the truth.

FRENEMY THIEF

Obama massively expanded the police state. We all feared a knock at our door and felt desperate.

I would rather take a political risk in pursuit of peace than risk peace in pursuit of politics. Trump

Friends are "enlightened" going along with sin yet dirty/who knows where they've been?

Obama had a way of treating same sex marriage as if Jesus himself would approve/he was shrewd.

Trump is helping blacks more than any other president has.

The democrats have embraced violence by the mere fact Maxine Watters has not been silenced.

You may have power with the people, then you won't. Think about that when feeling arrogant.

They're socialist activists, not journalists.

It's hard to make people stop hating when they have invested their whole life in this tragedy.

I was thinking such dark things/vain imaginings and now it's all perfect/divine again, imagine that.

Forget acting ability, transgenders should get every role in Hollywood due to their sexual identity?

It's not where there's smoke there's fire when they're creating the narrative calling us liars.

To go out and beat up conservatives is their new way to make friends and socialize afterwards.

FRENEMY THIEF

Civilization decay comes when the natural order is eliminated and all become degenerate.

While liberals are perpetually/professionally offended on behalf of others, the right is better.

Have faith we're winning the war tho' at the time it's hard losing jobs, family, income, whatever.

They keep going back to find dirt on him but he keeps moving forward/modern day Sansom.

If they get control and wipe out free speech we'll never again be able to get good men in like He.

CNN has lower ratings than the food network--ha ha condign punishment for those jerks.

America's the greatest country this side of heaven and we're losing it through complacency, nappin'

CNN doesn't report the news it fabricates it with fake parking lot scenes and we're all disgusted.

You don't go to heaven/avoid hell cuz you have talent ya know.

There's no such thing as racism, homophobism or sexism there's only good and evil, friends.

They made up words to control--so overcome it, love what's right and love God with all your might.

Anti-male Antifa are ruthless felons, perverts and lunatics armed to the teeth to destroy America.

FRENEMY THIEF

From their lowminds they jealously see him as a millionaire looking down on/telling em what to do.

The hip hop craze came over everyone thinking it's hip to be bad and now it's catastrophe/death.

I know you wanna kill em but be kind to diffuse the anger while stating boldly on all matters.

How dare you say you love your president. How dare you say meeting with Putin wasn't treason. Whoopi

In dense generations the intelligent aren't even nerds, just alien.

Art is to edify not to disgust/make us wanna die.

Trump could find a cure for cancer and they'd hate him for sure.

No matter what they'll never be chic--just don't have it, make wrong decisions, mentally effete.

Socialist lures: We'll fill your coffers even abort your kids ok just sit on your couch and vote as libs.

Cortez's views: socialist wrapped in ignorance. Cortez risk: Slash military and tax the rich.

Envy, theft, jealousy, covetousness, murder: that's socialism tho' its couched in sweet looks like her.

There's no such thing as good government, just limited or unlimited government.

All closed communities are the same: It's ok to lie to outsiders if it furthers their own game.

FRENEMY THIEF

Unless you say you hate Trump you're not part of the club, that's Hollywood.

Obama showed a disturbing but crystal-clear pattern of defending black racism towards white folks.

Millennials understood: Dictator killed millions = good. Offensive words = you're a no-good hood.

They don't have it, cannot come up with it, a blank slate--mimicry/slogans was all they had of late.

Disputing the liberal stance has been heretical for decades. They'd get mad and we'd concede.

Left is aghast we'd ever question the unquestionable so get strong and stand against the rabble.

Brainwashed by a theory showing them as morally superior, of course they can't let it go sir.

They don't think, they run an ideology in their head and accept the output without question.

It's not only debauched it's low class and gross. Walk away gently, nip it in the bud/, be boss.

No depth, no originality yet they hang on to dead themes unthinkingly.

There is no "obvious consensus" against Trump just a mass brainwash and social hypnotic.

Propaganda is not news.

FRENEMY THIEF

How can male feel good if his heritage is seen as repressive patriarchy? Left creates tragedy.

The normal competitive male drive is put down as tyrannical so how can he truly succeed or go on?

Take kids from school if hearing words "equity, inclusivity, white privilege or systemic racism"

Close school they're not being educated but indoctrinated and there's no excuse for it.

The left no longer considers us as fellow citizens but inferior or not even human. It's a war, amen.

They won't listen to facts, reason, logic or anything else disputing their views that we're all one.

I'm calling on God who is using Donald Trump. We can now see His plan to defeat the dumb.

Because we're in the right we're entirely spiritually connected: those are the patriots.

Riot is the voice of the unheard: Maxine Waters endorsing mob violence.

It's white privilege to call for civility. CNN

Trump has the power and courage of God within. It's so amazing to see it, America's best friend.

How can Trump have lunch with one who has just attacked him? Cuz he's not angry, it's nothing.

FRENEMY THIEF

Before a liberal speaks he surveys the lay of the land, a good man speaks from heart without a plan.

Donald Trump has to tweet cuz the children of the lie (the media) block it so he must speak it.

Obama had full power of the state and he took that power and destroyed everything in his wake.

Run like you're going to lose or prepare to concede.

When Barrack Obama came in it pushed republicans far right and Cortez will do the same, alright?

Fake news needs a new Obama so they'll overlook her extreme views and the destruction too.

So moral clarity lies in programs that are completely untenable and will never be paid for?

To Cortez, Trump's an "authoritarian hyper-capitalist"

It's very easy to virtue signal about policies that have no impact as they're never implemented.

Trudeau's brave new world of freedom, equality, inclusivity makes many Canadians swing far right.

Taught to sin but smile. Cumbaya generation is bright colors hiding disgusting darkness so vile.

The biggest tax cuts in American history and they still hate him, what a mystery.

FRENEMY THIEF

When in power they were kind/tolerant but lose power and their claws come out/they run amuck.

The America they envision is a curse. It was fantastic but they've made everything so much worse.

It was the democrats that interned the Japanese in WWII. Yes, weird despicables, it is you.

Out of liberal altruism you let everyone (and their mama) in and that's why you're not evolving.

Raised to be social they only feel comfortable surrounded by people but this is evil, just be real.

What ruined our hopes, dreams, lives? This social thing advanced in schools/filled with lies.

As usual Obama trashed our Founders from way back when and ditched our safety for left wing spin.

By Obama's abuse of certain laws he triggered social transformation without representation.

Ban the press dinner. The reprobate liberal mind is infinitely disgusting: depthless evil sinners.

Law and a godless moral code cannot protect us from evil. It's easier to ban guns from the people.

INFERIOR: Progressive underground/sixties sexual movement and anti-tradition counter culture.

God creates from nothing by the word of God alone, but they deny that making their own throne.

FRENEMY THIEF

Schools took prayer out and sex in. Overnight America changed as God was replaced by Satan.

Brainwash, lose compass: Only God is stable: why we need the Highest.

Kids go to school and they can't think logically. Can't drill down, expound, learn--a cultural tragedy.

They want your children to turn em into an animal that hates God and disrespects you/the law.

To stick to the gospel gotta expound on what's happening so we can adapt to this thing.

Drudge: smut standup shocks DC--went way too far this time, you see.

It's easy to get hooked on the internet as they line up similar suggestions so you choose from it.

We are religious, the bible calls them sodomites so we call them sodomites.
Russian Clergy

Trump's victory showed Russia there are two Americas but they only respect the conservatives.

I just love seeing the new nasty vile comics fall flat on their face. Ha ha what a total disgrace.

Left dressed up in tux/deluxe to celebrate bullying, vulgarity and hate and that's how the left wrecks.

The WHCD comedy standup was tasteless, aggressively unfunny and very sad.
Laura Ingraham

FRENEMY THIEF

Weak are taken in by the flashy evil Hollywood creeps but God rewards the humble, His peeps.

A filthy comedian is but a reflection of hatred for tradition, Trump and decent Americans.

To the loving left Michelle Wolf was not vile. This is how they talk to each other, that's their style.

What they call comedy is now vile bullying. Tearing down nice people and all the while smiling.

They forgive without repentance over and again but then gossip all over town about them.

Forgiving without repentance creates murderers and it's done by little old ladies and fakers.

They forgive without repentance for the virtue signal dance then tell everyone and not by chance.

We're countering Obama who keeps saying "don't listen to them"

Pathological altruism: I will sell you my own children to avoid being called racist.

All cultures had slaves but Christians for shortest amount of time, treated them best and *ended it.*

They're cruel misjudgments held us down and took us back. We cowered in the face of this tactic.

Hardly anyone has the tools/facts to fight back. But I do and will give you ammunition against brats.

FRENEMY THIEF

I am very excited about my new book except it puts me in a dangerous situation telling the truth.

This all comes down to one thing: liberals thinking everyone is alike. That's the blind--take a hike.

Childhood propaganda limits the practical implementation of adult rationality. Stefan Molyneux

I don't need anger management I need to be rid of the people making me angry.

IRAN nuclear wasn't a treaty just an Obama agreement that trump overturned and now ended.

Only strength is charismatic you'll never make it part of a weak-kneed, nightmarish catastrophe.

Be magnetic and charismatic by standing up against this s**t not by being one with these evil twits.

How cruel they are to call you a racist, an immoral label! Practice now: "I am NOT a racist"/turn the tables.

Profanity is such a cheap shot just to be accepted by the sluts and slobs. Be rare, choose God.

Cut em some slack they've been held way back by media hacks and Satan's schools of lax/no facts.

They simply don't know what they're talking about: virtue signalers for life and you can't go back.

They think they're saving you but it's communism in a nice image and not Christian, so bid adieu.

Watch your obscene gestures too. It's debased an entire generation and powerfully subliminal.

FRENEMY THIEF

Aging baby boomers are the only thing holding the world together. When we die out, tragedy/horror.

It's a lost generation. They're lost cuz their grandparents were lost, the grossness is fixed.

It's almost like they speak another language, they're vulgar and illiterate but that's our kids.

Satan changes the image of God into his image and that explains the insanity you see at present.

Before you vote always ask if they approve of men going into girl's bathrooms. Cool fools.

When we fail God's able to instruct us. He that suffers has ceased from sin, the bible tells us.

I don't hate the youth it's what they've been taught, the problem is they ignore Jehovah God.

I don't hate the youth it's just how callous they've become. Think of the things they call fun!

I don't hate the youth it's just another realm altogether and they seem to want me gone, a dinosaur.

Calling us bigots: slogans/phrases you've learned by rote--can't think beyond lies you bought.

Us not dying out yet is the only thing keeping you from going over the edge /falling into sludge.

They programmed you thru your video games, what a bore you've become with nothing done.

FRENEMY THIEF

I don't see how you can stand being around all those you call church, they've fallen away sir.

The popular church is demonic, a den of thieves encouraging sin and it's contagious/traumatic.

They look good, decent, rich, cool and high but without Jesus/repentance demons are rife.

Of course they love a church who won't mention sin just to be your friend, the sinner loves em.

I don't have to attend, I already know cuz it won't mention sin.

The mark of the true church is how many people don't come back.

There's a lot of racist gangs of black people and the epitome is Mad Dog Maxine Waters: evil.

Trump gave billions to black scholarships and still the madwoman Maxine Waters bitches.

Ireland joins throw-away community of irreplaceable human beings through abortion on demand.

Antifa: Failure to Launch Syndrome or afraid of not having shelter (mommy's home)?

It's culture or sexual licentiousness, you can't have both. Stefan Molyneux

The truth is outlawed. Free the truth-teller from the UK criminals.

Your problem was getting involved with em in the first place cuz if they never met you, you'd be ok.

FRENEMY THIEF

This is a big social not a church, it would disgust and appall a (saintly) religious introvert.

Paul said no chattering in the church. The way you prattle in the sanctuary is irritating, a curse.

Bianci: what does she know, dressing like that and misleading children--a *religious* leader?

Outside forces have taken over churches as well as our country. It's a plan to kill religion/you/me.

If they knew who they were they'd be so bored with this! They must fill time or feel more lost.

Ireland was the last bastion of pro-life sentiment.

Nazi level tyranny: arresting those reporting on corruption then banning anyone telling about it.

Blacks want justice for everything but what about the whites who died to end slavery? Nothing

We react to demons in em, children of the lie call that racism but that all dissolves once we know em.

When slogans trump logic, we've reached the end and can't debate it--so just get to safety.

It's not racism they are judging evil: demons. It wasn't that way, they were well accepted not lemons.

It's not racism, they are judging evil: demons. It wasn't that way, they were well accepted not lemons.

FRENEMY THIEF

Kids won't learn critical thinking unless given both sides of the argument and they don't get that.

It's not tolerance, love or feel-good but about social deconstruction-- destroying our world.

It's not about feelings, they're exploiting your feelings as a billy club against our civilization.

It brings us to tears: them glorifying the destruction of social norms for thousands of years.

People are horrible so don't expect any better and you won't be disappointed.

Today we mourn those who died so we remain unharmed.

Bring on the authoritarianism, it's only bolstering and corroborating populist sentiments!

For race and sex equalists politics is personal. It's how they see themselves, just can't get real.

White Europeans like Shakespeare are now universal but native symbols are appropriation, cultural.

It's a blend of socialism and false Christianity.

So many call themselves Christians but are not.

If you don't read the news you're uninformed. If you read the news you're misinformed. Stefan Molyneux

Everyone is a racist and they don't even know it. That's their spiel and we're darn sick of it.

FRENEMY THIEF

When progressives win they impose weird stuff on ya. Real reality is natural but not in America.

Roseanne's better off, the show woulda turned: open borders Islamic crap, social justice warrior stuff.

Starbach's reeducation close: Virtue signaling by Soros who's behind it all.

Roseanne fallout shows why you never apologize to the left. And so maudlin-- that part I don't get.

To the extent their art is social justice type stuff Trump's victories only reveal their fluff.

Obama and Hillary shut down whole towns. Fredonia devastated next to me, all mines gone.

Their whole world was turned upside down, the ontologically fatal insight that they've lost ground.

Neo-liberal thought virus running rampant thru our culture: do not engage with "I'm not a racist".

The second you start to beg and prove your valor or virtue ("I'm not a racist") you've lost it.

When Roseanne met em half way she lost our support--apologizing to left is not like a victor.

We have a right to put people down/hurt feelings with our speech--they do, ten times worse ok.

The African American liberal always gets a pass, Roseanne does not even though she apologized.

FRENEMY THIEF

To a conservative it seems everyone is liberal or calls themselves conservative but not actual.

It's not about Roseanne but the double standard taking over the land: we can't speak but they can.

This isn't Christianity it's communism with virtue signaling.

He who departs from evil makes himself a prey and it's lack of justice that displeases God today.

Donald Trump is not a racist but a realist and a greenist: he wants prosperity for all of us.

Trash the 2nd amendment cuz we can't have armed pop and tyrannical government at the same time.

After the **FOXES** were dominant there's a return to the **LION** beginning with Donald Trump.

Academic Jihad: Rewriting history and reality, making everyone angry, inciting cultural suicide.

Miseducated/dangerous thinking--lawfare, litigation jihad: they don't like what you said, you've had it.

In fear of being sued, they shut up. No, not you but everyone else in terror will no longer talk.

When it comes to emotions/feelings they ignore the facts and logic has nothing to do with it.

White people love feeling good about themselves by feeling bad about being white. Jarad Taylor

FRENEMY THIEF

They move on you, take your privacy/solitude, demand you take others in (you've got room): REFUSE.

Donald Trump: the Great White Hope.

Equalize everything: male and female, and all races, are the same. Charming differences, gone.

Putin likes the ladies. He's not a soy boy, girlie man, buggery or silly tranny.

University is a free flow of ideas not safe spaces and deplatforming those with whom you disagree.

Censorship in academia is stifled truth in the name of feelings.

You say we're not destroyed? Look at our schools, look at California or Detroit, invasions overnight.

Us dinosaurs will be outa here and it'll all implode cuz you guys know nothing what Jesus spoke.

WHO were the ones who moved, enslaved or killed the American Indians? Democrats: Jacksonians.

Democrats took Indian land/gave it to white settlers in exchange for votes--it's always the rats, no?

One group of Americans (Dems) did terrible things and another group (Reps) stopped them.

Demo Frisco spends 30 million a year cleaning up fecal matter, needles and trash--it's so liberal!

"Equal and equitable outcome" means to debase whites cuz our IQ explains success out of sight.

FRENEMY THIEF

Modern art is coupled with sophistic explanations--that's ridiculous as it should stand on its own.

Wordy explanations of art means it's incomplete, didn't do it's job, picking up where you left off.

Did Michelangelo give explanations of his paintings or do they just stand on their own, scintillating?

You need wordy explanations of your art because it's so dull, ineffectual and nondescript?

Black men are whining like little girls about white people holding them back. Jesse Peterson

Black people are suffering--their men not worth a dime--due to family break down/moral slide.

I ask you where you're going and you tell me where you've been. Please answer the question.

Youth don't have maturity/brain power to see thru scams so hold your head up high/just ignore em.

Insane crazy brainwashed kids actually want open borders and say racism exists so I say: be rid.

Feel pity (despite fear of violence) for these crazy kids who can't think and push you to the brink.

Dumb kids not aware/don't care how illegals destroy black jobs, slaughter animals or kill our pets.

Kids have suffered such a cramdown of insanity I say: round em all up and bring em back to reality.

THE END OR A BEND

The Great White Replacement

It's not an immigration crisis but a 17 year old UN plan (2000) called the "Great People Replacement". Refugee quotas is about one thing: 21st century invasion and subjugation of the West, you think? The enemy of my enemy is my friend--liberals love anyone who hates white America. Lord, come again! They're degrading us to third world levels, crashing economy and culture through invasion by vultures. We the best stand in their way of global governance so they must level and homogenize the west. Are they coming in to supported the aged (the stated reason) or get these entitlements themselves? Consolidate European countries so they may be subsumed under global governance, that's it. They create wars for a massive pretext to bring people in and they'll continue to: that's the plan. The UN agenda is horrific but the EU sanctions are nothing compared to threats from migrants. Empires have been trying to stop the American system for 241 years. No worries, Trump is here.

THE END OF A BEND?

It's not an immigration crisis but a 17 year old UN plan (2000) called the "Great People Replacement".

You don't want to see how laws or sausage is made. Bismarck

They're degrading us to third world levels, crashing economy and culture through invasion by vultures.

We the best stand in their way of global governance so they must level and homogenize the west.

Are they coming in to supported the aged (the stated reason) or get these entitlements themselves?

Consolidate European countries so they may be subsumed under global governance, that's it.

They create wars for a massive pretext to bring people in and they'll continue to: that's the plan.

The UN agenda is horrific but the EU sanctions are nothing compared to threats from migrants.

Refugee quotas is about one thing: 21st century invasion and subjugation of the West, you think?

Since climate-deniers are older--and scared--"we're just gonna have to wait for em to die". Bill Nye

The enemy of my enemy is my friend--liberals love anyone who hates white America. Lord, come again!

Empires have been trying to stop the American system for 241 years. No worries, Trump is here.

THE END OF A BEND?

 Globalism is falling but what to do about the populations invading?

Obama, Hillary, McCain are the modern founders of ISIS but Trump is bad for clearing the crisis?

ISIS is falling fast, very fast. Donald Trump

We're entering a new dark age: they're gonna reduce your populations and control all that you say.

Obituary data bases then bussing people to vote ten times: that's voter fraud by democrats (slime).

They think globally: the world's a chessboard. They don't care about us but we have the dear Lord.

Think what woulda happened had Hillary got in: WWIII, take guns and millions immigrants flooding.

Stakes never higher: If globalists win they have the technology to destroy our freedom, ever again.

The will of the people doesn't matter as the places for whites in London get smaller and smaller.

They're not trying to reform Islam but taking the worst and most brutal as their shock troops: bam!

Left doesn't care about "diversity" just bringing them em in to vote for their agenda: death/immorality.

End the lie of diversity which is just to get white votes for stupidity.

The left who was in love with Russia when held by communism now say "do not talk to them".

THE END OF A BEND?

Illegal border crossings down 70%, arrests up 40%: under trump we're back/he's made a serious dent.

Sanctuary cities are just symbolic: They have no power nor authority and Trump's proving it daily.

Under Obama when ICE stood down they imported 3 million in eight years--but ICE is back, no tears!

Globalists have shifted to Islam as the main religion thinking to use them as a battering ram.

Globalists hate two things: Americans and Christians.

89% Muslims believe in murder for apostasy.

Not just a clash of cultures but of civilizations.

How could you possibly think everyone is equal? They defecate in streets but the Americans are evil?

31,000 Muslim terror attacks since 911.

Trump has killed ISIS but does that really end the crisis? NO, it's a 17-year U.N. plan to REPLACE US.

Russia advances Christianity, free market politics and battling radical Islam.

The huddled masses were meant to work not sit on their fat asses.

Huddled masses yearning to be free weren't meant to go to the front of the line/push out you and me.

They push Americans down so the illegal immigrant goes ahead, wearing a crown.

THE END OF A BEND?

We all love a merit-based system except for corrupt liberal politicians living off their votes, labor, whatever.

Mass population exchanges like this were never seen in history except in conquered nations: tragedies.

Mass deportations common in the ancient world. Cut off from homeland they were easiest to control.

The culture/traditions of the former population disappears and along with that their liberty (tears).

Are the liberal elites forcing these policies on us evil, dumb or detached while destroying our liberty?

The populations and cultures of the west are being artificially and fundamentally changed.

By being replaced, we won't be able to resist the immigrant hordes and unelected globalist boards.

Read "Trump's War", Michael Savages--on the evil results of ancient mass population exchanges.

We can no longer take in your wretched refuse from your teaming shore--we want no more!

We can no longer take in your homeless, tempest-tossed cuz we have our own and have a new boss.

Groups getting rich off the multi-billion dollar immigration scam: You'd be shocked to know all of em.

Why are billionaires in favor of open borders?

THE END OF A BEND?

How refreshing: A leader who puts his national identity above his race and who loves you and me.

An international group owning high-end facilities for illegals in every country, making billions honey.

Most Americans want illegal immigration stopped, special interests don't and thus America rots.

Making billions off illegal aliens living in luxury resorts, enjoyin': pirates benefitting from hordes, stealin'.

Why hordes of immigration? Big business, big government and big religion all with one mission!

Big business, government and religion making a bundle all off of your back: the patriots seen as trivial/sad sacks.

We all want (very few oppose) a merit-based immigration system except the evil plans of globalism.

Politically impossible to do the right thing: ban immigration for seven years (no more public pissing).

1965 Immigration Reform Act: drunken Kennedy let us drown in this war as mistress did in her car.

Time to limit immigration with a merit-based English-speaking system.

Pres. Trump ran on immigration control, don't forget that. He wants to please us, his electorate.

Follow the money to understand: those who oppose his immigration plan.

THE END OF A BEND?

Root out all immigration attorneys–the poison in our system: parasites with law degrees crippled this country.

Hordes were brought into ancient countries to destroy them–to remake demographics/control em.

They conquer you by letting strange hordes in--millions not just a few. Save America: no immigration lawyers too.

By separating invading people from their homelands the new country can more easily control them.

Africans coming from tribal societies are resistant to democracy. They don't even understand it, see?

Radical liberal feminists taking over Sicily, as the men are driven out replaced by migrant bullies.

Old Sicily: liberty and local self-government. New Sicily: hordes get jobs, all-ok with central globalment.

As you learn to put your nation above your race, then you'll be an American my son and progress.

"Immigration" lawyer means they're gaming the system, sir.

1/4 of all terror attacks are by teens: fact.

These invaders have no ties to their new land, no willingness to defend it--from who, them?

No one can support the billions wanting to come here and live off he fat of the land from gullible chumps.

THE END OF A BEND?

The poor shall be endless. There has never been equality and never will be and some will be blessed.

For many of those the dream is over but for us, our dreams are just beginning to manifest.

Barry invaded his nation with diseased immigrants.

Illegal immigration down 71% under Trump.

There is no such thing as equality but the gullible believe it/create tragedy.

Government was literally dissolving a people and electing a new one.

Higher IQ countries care about contracts and private property, low IQ--not so much/not their reality.

The essential for capitalism to work is truthfulness, and most third world cultures have none of this.

Free market, small government, separation of church and state vs. what they are used to: hate.

Multiculturalism is the top of "approved think" and white is the lowest stink.

It's a globalist plan--for 17 years talking about replacing populations and now it's happened.

"America, look at the UK: Don't be us." Katie Hopkins

They go to London, they don't mix--it's not multicultural, it's balkanization and culture clash stress.

"Multiculturalism" is a lie, a disconnect, a mis-truth and they know it too.

What could be more important than helping your culture by learning all of this--see it all, focus.

THE END OF A BEND?

Do not look to western Europe, we don't want that--hold your head up!

They want to bring in low IQ populations so they'll vote democrat.

What creeps--after the church service they go to see amputations.

Both globalists and the vatican are publicly allied with Islam.

New litmus test: Share Infowars, you're fired.

Their time is short: Globalism is totally unelected, authoritarian and deeply allied with radical Islam.

Trump drove a stake through heart of globalism along with China/the EU but they're telling you he's pooh.

Twisted: BBC says women should wear burkas to prove they're feminists.

He's defeating ISIS, when our government had been openly backing them and turning them loose.

Do you know how much the globalists hate you? Come to your senses and support Trump too.

You've gotta be ALL IN or the globalists win.

BBC pushing burkas to show you're mature, force-feeding manure

Dems are coming to their senses, switching to just-miss the floods coming in--disaster IMMINENT.

We don't want em here!

There is much evil in the world and Trump's trying to make it right so American dreams can unfurl.

THE END OF A BEND?

Of course they fear Russian-American collusion—because it's ultra important.

Globalists hate Putin who's been reforming, cutting oligarchs, empowering family, fighting for Christianity.

Putin protests their anti-human plans and that's why globalists hate the man.

All over the world they're rising up against the antiChristian spirit of enslavement: global government.

The globalist's saying Russia is enemy number one deflects from the real crimes they commit.

They'll do anything to destroy enemies of world government.

A realistic, practical leader who refuses globalization is hated.

Trump is trying to take the globalist foot off our neck but is blocked by the sold-out/corrupt.

Purging anyone talking against globalism or how it's allied with Islam or not for a war with Russia.

TTP and the carbon tax has been killed, 69% illegals reduced, 4 trillion stocks up, million new jobs.

Globalist's satanic plan: separate humans from their essence while they get the best/don't pay taxes.

The globalists try to intimidate him by false hoaxes and accusation of Russian intervention.

Putin is obstacle to globalization and that's why they hate him

All over the world it's the spirit of Christ rising up against this evil, callous, controlling globalist spirit.

THE END OF A BEND?

Globalists and Islam are on the same side in the battle against the west, the best.

Putin is the mythologically crucial "Defender" of Christianity, tradition, sovereignties and families.

Not inclined to follow theories but naturally conservative, Christian, familial, defender of the loyal.

He is Russian not cosmopolitan, A nation-lover not a world traveler.

It's a return to common sense: cultural nationalism with a Christian base.

South African white farmers killed every day and since they have the expertise they're all gonna starve

They wanna protest something and it's easy from their lack of understanding.

Populists reflect humanity, globalists wanna change humanity.

Aren't out to get their country due to a sense of roots and not being sold out.

Every defender of the president is cut-off.

Being normal is a heroic act.

Anti-family stuff together with the ugly art and buildings is the same spirit of tyranny and disintegrating.

Exchange all links with collective identity.

Gender nature must be overcome, controlled and destroyed?

"Don't say men and women, that's hurtful to others"--huh?

"Exchange all links with collective identity"--sends chills up my spine, communitarianism the enemy.

THE END OF A BEND?

When you feel abandoned you're playing victim. Be in control: see them ALL (every one) as irrelevant.

About carnality you'll have great remorse.

The mark of a great teacher is all those who don't come back.

FRENEMIES

Not a victim, you kept yourself in that position.

May the Lord cut off all flattering lips and the tongues that speak proud boasting. Psalms 12: 3

The empty-headed fool says in his heart: there is no God. They are corrupt, none doeth good. Psalm 14: 1

Smiling fools have many friends who can't think deeply and just wanna feel life makes some sense.

Keep reversing matrices. Brutal reversals mark discovery.

Giving/taking in marriage, events, selfies, that is the human race.

Social world is timing, events and selfies. The inner world is timeless space, inspiration, artistries.

Everybody has their heyday when people listen to them.

Outer entertainment gets you through the rough spots but ultimately it's just you and nothing else.

THE END OF A BEND?

Life is a pie. For every moment you do that you can't do this, your destiny and God's blessing/kiss.

Music is absolutely the highest when the mind is the freest cuz with movies you gotta track and focus.

For every moment you're concentrating on a movie you coulda been doing your own thing, focusing.

I could never give a darn about your freakin' club, I got my own high end thing galaxies ahead of ya.

Only musica for highest day ever, love ya

You're not a writer if you don't make a dent, if you're not READ so that's part of it--is it fluff instead?

Stay spiritual by saying NO to the carnal. Sure you gotta eat and procreate but please: use restraint!

Be unconcerned when you see the wicked flourishing fast cuz they're soon mowed down like grass.

FAME: It's not an ego thing, it's a necessity. Think about that and now you must prepare for it.

We want to see justice done cuz that's a main attribute of God.

We're told to be happy for em but know how wicked they are so we lean on the promise in God's word.

Vindication is necessary for the relief of the saints. Vindicate: make things right Lord/please don't wait!

A true genius never trusts his memory. Albert Einstin

THE END OF A BEND?

Love needs so great, nothing fills the tank. Without God, addictions reign despite being spanked.

Men's minds are full of boxes that don't touch each other, to compartmentalize "I'll do that later".

Women's minds are totally interconnected so everything means everything, the one basis for arguing.

Everything from California's in a bag to throw out. My life started here as I adapt to new environments.

They can always find you another way but blocking causes them inconvenience and that's okay.

A proven link between unhealed trauma and physical or mental illness, so focus on that for realness.

Depression: Not just sadness, the brain stops.

Likes = addiction. Just enjoying you day: release of all affliction.

Left to their own devices without God: they fail, crash and burn due to vices and being so flawed.

Her life was stultified and broken from unhealed trauma: angry and brazen but that's the reason.

If you can heal from that terrible trauma of being locked in a box or whatever you will be the best, ever.

People are cruel cuz they're consciences are seared cuz they adapted to those without empathy dear.

Return to the terrible trauma, work on that.

THE END OF A BEND?

It got so I couldn't talk to anyone they all made me sick. People are weird from accepting this stink.

Mental illness is a curse, splitting body from mind, God and universe.

Growing up takes tears and unlearning things takes years.

Archetypes determine how fairytales and psychodramas are played out--we are owned by them, no doubt.

Archetypes are in levels from fool to king. Repent then it's a higher one you'll naturally be choosing.

You don't like what I do, go--I can't adapt to you

No, we're not "nice". It's about being real and telling the truth--that it's your evil we despise.

Depending on your money and not on God = holes in your bucket and being seen as odd, flawed.

I came to fire the whole staff and I sometimes use colorful language. Scaramucci

In private that's how guys talk but in society may be better not to use colorful language, ok we get it.

These people here, they are country folk bumpkins and I think we should get to know them.

These people here, I never see em cuz we're all patriots into our own thing but we'd protect them.

You're to be bold in righteousness not timid and weak from sin your highness.

Rich think they get outa anything by throwing money at it but find it's not true: holes in their bucket.

THE END OF A BEND?

If you're meant to be together nothing can hold you apart. Just rely on God's pull and continue to work.

It's not that we wanna see em suffer but rather see justice cuz that's God's attribute/gift to us.

I look at some in my ancestry: they all had their heyday but got old, died and went to hell anyway.

Once you see the light they all look so foolish. They can't see their peculiar looking caricatures.

How do I know how I'll feel on that day/hour? I can't make commitments, I'd rather be inspired.

Retirement is like slipping into cozy pajamas. Falling outa structure into God's phantasmagoria.

Don't try to be cute, watch what you say and it's best to say nothing, ok?

Need fame to make a dent.

Stop following lower elements--anchors holding you down and your relapse occurs in increments.

Turn away if you sense the slightest bit of sultriness, carnality, too closeness or info on their mess.

It should relieve you to know it was demons. You're only blame was weakness which let em in.

Sin leaves a muddy aura, a disheveled appearance, dirty, unkempt--except with the psychopath.

Religion is a fowl spirit. Faith and relationship is what God gave us and with miracles we know it.

THE END OF A BEND?

PTSD: You only suffer after the trauma is over—the body's defense against bad emotional killers.

Let no one tell you how to conduct yourself. Let the word only tell you or from grace you will fall.

END is not decline but your peak. Stop thinking it's over--you've never been better/more unique.

They've made it big so we can't put em down, even though obvious sinners and dead wrong?

You don't have it in you, ok? You just don't have it, you STINK but with a little work and humility...

Fat, dumpy, grungy, not-quite clean, gross, hypnotized, unrefined, mean.

If you're a writer you're always writing. If you're a "writer" you never write but may be pretending?

They are mentally ill, that's why they act that way. I've been in that state of vulnerability: easy to sway.

All the kids are so nice no need to tell em twice.

"Publishers" will mess with your work. Do a PDF (as YOU want it), go to printer than hire marketer.

You were smart enough to make a marriage work so had the protection to apply yourself/get the perks.

Never fear loss of relevance enough to compete with youth. They know nothing and are uncouth.

To be with God is total power but in sin that power is withdrawn and life turns sour, a wilted flower.

THE END OF A BEND?

What the world thinks is of no consequence. Relate to God, angels, seasons, family and pets.

Don't be disturbed over when you mimicked the cultural neurosis of filthiness, it's just emptiness.

Forces of evil assembling against you NOT of God but cuz we live in the enemy's camp, seen as odd.

Recall sweet tragedies: when evil sought to overcome me but God swooped down and saved me.

You liberal virtue-signaling friends have become worse, more obdurate. Reject now and get with it.

Stop feeling bad cuza what the dumbed liberal said. It's a powerful social hypnotic and it's red.

Stop feeling bad when they're prospering and you're not. It's a temporary thing before eternal rot.

You're so good, so high, that no one notices. You're so deep and so fast they just can't process it.

Your group doesn't understand you so of course you feel hated or odd, so get with those who love God.

Forces of evil assembling against you not of God but cuz we live in the enemy's camp we're seen as odd.

If they lack discernment they'll make lousy and devastating decisions for your life so detach, revive.

You created the monsters by being liberal and not drawing lines. They got worse, you lost your mind.

THE END OF A BEND?

Whosoever shall gather together against thee shall fall for thy sake. Isaiah 54: 15

They don't care, they never think of you and make no room for you: is this your family and friends too?

Since when is a buzzcut unfeminine? It is worn by beautiful rockstars and admired by gentlemen.

Wipe em from your mind and replace with Jesus. Do this every time and soon there's no more crisis.

Stress can throw you over the edge then you start acting insane, but all goes well when you relax again.

I'm like a drag queen--I love to dress and wear make up! Isn't it strange how everything is mixed up.

Many women have "frog fur" for hair. Make it easy--you'd look so much better in a buzzcut, I swear.

Well, sick. Sick, well. It's a sliding variable depending on the stimulus--the chemicals or toxic smells.

I'm not into that, I'm a Christian. So don't act like it's normal and push it on me cuz it's sick man.

To be creatively aligned with God and do His will you must be strong, like working for 3 days long.

You act like it's normal just cuz we've been hammered with it but all that brainwashing was not legit.

Why is long stringy matted greasy/dry split-end hair feminine? Cuz it's all about the image, man.

THE END OF A BEND?

God says He has plans to prosper you so have faith, do your work and as for critics, tell em shut up.

By redefining sin and leaving the possibility open, you're drawing innocent people in/it's disabling.

It's just something to do to fill time till I die.

They know nothing and have no real values, they've been so brainwashed to accept the blues.

Since your wisdom dies with you, get to work. It's God's goals you're accomplishing, it will have perks.

If you love God you'll stay away from that sort of thing cuz it's truly sickening.

WHY long hair? I see it in the food, on the bathroom floor/everywhere but the truly chic are rare.

Cuz your circle tells you how great you are, you get worse and worse: not a star but very below par.

They think you're just an older anyway (odd tragedy) so let em go and get into your DESTINY.

Thank God for the people lesson, even tho' it meant treachery, loss, invasion, theft, deception.

Is that a cheesecake smile? To heck with you: be sober, be vigilant, avoid levity/run the last mile.

Seek out old posts and you won't find them now. It's as if they're not the same person, I know.

Irresistibly you will now be a success and there's not a thing you can do to stop it/cause a mess.

THE END OF A BEND?

Don't waste your breath any more with people, conserve your energy, stay with those in True Reality.

When it comes to the gospel, family and friends are laid aside.

If they talk to you that way drop em and ban em that's all you can do ma'am.

It is not true that whatever we see "out there" is in us first. That is typical BS from occultists.

If you're that good destiny will find you: the lake fills up/finds it's closest outlet, so now just cruise.

The greatest work you could ever do is showing these kids how stupid they are. Do it, create it: be a star.

Free-will makes you sloppy with too many options. Calvinism brings restraint and then opulence.

If my highest groove is predestined and in my imagination I still must attain it through elimination.

You're not gonna find the highest groove as a sensual sinner. You must repent to attain/be a winner.

Free will leaves too much room for sin and evil imaginations. Stay in the groove of predestinations.

Keep it simple or it's too much unnecessary trivia we don't need to know--it obscures the point.

Stay spiritual by saying NO to the carnal. Sure you gotta eat and procreate but please: use restraint.

Atrazine in the water changes the sex of amphibians.

THE END OF A BEND?

We can't be drawn back into this defiling dietary doctrine but that's what Satan wants and it's sin.

A new obsession in the church: diet/health programs stealing our great inheritance and it stinks.

Don't be a sucker falling for church-dieting hook line and sinker cuz it's the devil Satan the stinker.

Diet isolates/rigidifies, you don't follow God's edicts and won't listen to what He says about it.

Since many churches talk of diet it's proof how far we've fallen for God calls it hypocrisy/leaven.

Nothing more sickening than a not-quite-clean restaurant. When you go out, use discernment.

Greasy (fatty) spoons and sticky spoons (lowfat food but unclean rooms), going back no time soon.

No more restaurants cuz we don't know what's in it and we never feel good the next day darn it!

Soy, cornstarch, gum, wood, sugar, corn syrups, bugs, GMO: it's all in the food making us ugly and old.

Don't tell me restaurants are good when I bloat for two days, there's always something I wouldn't use.

"Eat whatever's put in front of you"--can't do this. I get sick just thinking of it, credit it to age I guess

The law is death and condemnation not in Christ so don't be defiled by dietary law, that's the gist.

THE END OF A BEND?

When it comes to the booze there's no in-between if genetic and that's the great lesson for ascetics.

Sure, I'd love to have a beer once in awhile but I KNOW--and refuse, cuz I look back at hell below.

In my great ancestry they either died in the gutter or became great orators: boozers or tea-totalers.

Vainly puffed up in their fleshly minds, not holding fast to Christ from which health is sustained.

Diet is a form of witchcraft promoted in the church to it's shame--even Nazi dictators did the same.

Not only is diet an expensive and pointless deception, it will defile you into bondage away from God.

I can feel so good, then suddenly lousy. It's from chemicals which are rife everywhere/get drowsy.

First reaction: acid. Then vertigo, dizziness, nausea, can't put head up, coma, casket: it's classic.

Cuz your sick suddenly or well suddenly your family may say you're faking it, another snake pit.

Chemical sensitivity causes mental illness too. So not only are you sick they wanna lock up the shrew.

Fasting: Height-width ratio changed, cranial enlarged, physiognomy realigned, tone purified.

If I eat noodles/veg or tacos I'm good for 24 hours but if animal I grow saddlebags/love handles.

Fruit, noodles or tacos. Can't eat animal, that's just me folks.

THE END OF A BEND?

Feelings of abandonment can come from chemical sensitivity-- that was quite an insight to me.

MCS: So it's a limbic system problem, over-reactions increase sensitivity so gotta rewire the brain.

The average state in the west is to age very ungracefully but ignore what you see, it doesn't have to be.

It's a doctor's duty to protect you for those who do wrong: that's big pharma and diet all along.

Nutrition is the most powerful tool to attain cessation of the aging process: think of that, success!

There's something wrong with their faces: lopsided, conflicted.

The more inflammation in your system the more pain with age but there's a one-third drop going vegan.

Chipmunk cheeks says she loves the ketogenic diet but there's something wrong and she can't deny it.

So much aging is just closing-in arteries. Now de-age by unclogging through fruits and veggies.

The highest therapy is to eat once a day and tacos do it, don't even want any more fruit before it.

TACOS: it's all RAW, the lettuce, onions, tomatoes and cilantro. Yum, tortilla/cheese or avocado.

Rice noodles are great as a backup or storage. But it's still cooked and compared to tacos, boring.

THE END OF A BEND?

Marital arguments/rage are another result of chemical sensitivity, so when you get mad, go easy.

It's the fact I can do 24 hours fast after tacos. They give me that: satiety, delicious, wholesome.

The greatest part is the raw salsa: all cleansing, acid-binding, rejuvenating and the best: RAW.

The tortilla is cooked, big deal. It all goes through and is real.

One meal: Tacos please cuz it's all raw except for tortillas and cheese.

LIBERALISM EVEN IN CHURCHES

Left isn't fighting bigotry, they are it's greatest defenders.

If I dress in a kimono that's "cultural misappropriation": it's liberal theories causing this commotion.

There are thousands of sins and that's one of them.

It's just not true that trannies commit suicide cuz we say women aren't men and men aren't women.

Rape and incest occur 2% of the time but are used as an abortion excuse 98% of the time.

Trannies impose the necessity of fictionalized thinking on society.

Calling a male a male is now "aggressively insulting" and calling a female a female also needs censuring.

Police killings of blacks down 70% in 30 years.

Just cuz someone's against the left doesn't mean he's conservative--e.g. Milo or the addicted.

THE END OF A BEND?

People saw through things like Hillary and the Bushes and along with Trump said "we're sick of this".

Whoever cheers him the loudest becomes his top advisor?

Removing a president outside of impeachment is illegal but the democrats are calling for it, wow.

Traitors will always fire those saying the left's aligned with Soros and Islam.

Hillary hysterical so Barry said "Let him get in, claim he's a Russian later--this is too dangerous".

FOX: Backhanded or sneak attacks on the president, going along with stuff, opposition control.

Look behind things, get to bottom of it. Genius looks at cycles, systems, layers, how they spin it.

The elite want a robot like Hillary: they want that coldness like a military.

Men wimped by feminists may even get off on cultural gang rapists.

Fake news has failed, they've had their waterloo. But the elites still want the facade despite low views.

The media has no more legitimacy, they're just a disruptive force disabling the patriots like you and me.

Revolutionary, trailblazing, rebirth: That's the Trump presidency in three words. Alex Jones

90% donations to RINOS/noecons are by dems.

For people so smart--the right universities, the right politics--they are so dumb don't you think?

THE END OF A BEND?

What to do: celebrate they fired you, banned your book, made you look a kook cuz that's what it took.

Times of transition are high synchronicity (magic coincidences) and much of it's on facebook I think.

This Whitehouse is interested in what we evangelicals believe. This is of great importance: a reprieve!

Christians have great impact on Trump's policies. Think of that after the most dirty rat in recent history.

The rainbow is a sign to the world that God's word is true. So take it back from those perverse few.

Destruction of the Canaanites was not an attack on the innocent but God's judgment of abomination.

FBI is the distilled essence of corruption.

For all their criminal activity they come off like regular guys with style, so see through them as has Alex and Milo.

It won't be a civil war between two organized armies, but lone wolf terrorists crushed as anomalies.

They hate Christians who trigger consciences long dead. Why not repent, since Jesus was bled?

You warn em not to do it, they do it and get ripped off then never talk to you again--what a laugh.

We give the same vote to one who isn't smart, is dependent on the state and never reads a book.

THE END OF A BEND?

Since God created us male and female the transgender is the ultimate rebellion and destined to fail.

As Christians we have authority to bind and loose so pray or America dies/becomes the caboose.

Our president is fascinated by the plight of ordinary Christian folk that government ignored/saw as a joke.

Ignore the media, friends--he's moving so fast it makes your head spin.

Family and friends we're onto you. Face it: On the wrong side for decades thinking you were cool.

Obama recruited transgenders, put them in military then made government pay for a social experiment.

In a dangerous world the transgender soldier gets 90 day leave for the operation costing $200,000.

Did "change" mean transgender surgery? Yep, cuz it was Obama so that's no longer a mystery.

Obama ruin-a-nation: "Hey friends, join the military and we'll change for your sex change operation".

Anytime you have the same sex together it attracts homo predators.

Caveat: Don't send your kids to camp and no sleepovers, for gay sex hookups are everywhere.

Gays joke about hook-ups for sex. Promiscuity is its greatest characteristic and Milo knows this.

Kids/parents: Watch for older peers who are corrupt already with perverseness/pornography.

THE END OF A BEND?

White men: You didn't do anything wrong so stop apologizing--ignore the social warrior demoralizing.

Liberals have more freedom with Christians in charge.

Milo may hate the left but is not a conservative, cuz Milo talks of gay sex hookups in superlatives.

We've come so far in the information war, they're a huge joke/no brainer but nevertheless, persevere.

If they take away our speech rights, it's game over--they win cuz we can't tell em what's happening.

Sexual freedom (anarchy) for them is a loss of religious freedom for us.

We have a president who is not afraid to take on the failed policies of the previous administration.

I don't get to use the government as a club against you cuz I don't like what you say/pray a different way.

You talk about rude speech but it's ok for Hillary to insult middle class citizens as deplorable you say?

To prove they are feminists they get mean thinking it's tough but to real men it's an unnatural scene and a putoff.

If gays are into hookups, lesbians are about control. They get really mean in a borrowed masculine role.

No camps/sleepovers cuz those kids are already highly sexualized but unknown until it is night.

They see primitive as superior and advanced as depraved but the former have a dark underbelly, not ok.

THE END OF A BEND?

True conservatism is not just being against the left but about decency and that's a no-brainer truly.

Older feminists talking that vulgar way so casually--they are witches and so unattractive, really.

Children taught the "fun" of being around drag queens. Perverse like Sodom and Gomorrah, only worse.

He's giving us time to repent before nation is destroyed. He's withholding judgment, that's why.

How long will God allow it to go on: America's sodomites defiling children?

Older females are supposed to instill youth morals not act like carnival barkers and sluts themselves.

It's all fluff: smiles, whistles and demons. They'll be mowed down like the grass despite having class.

It hurts to be banned by the whole group but that's how it works, don't you know the scoop?

The foolish virtue signaling of the entire Hollywood left is so boring, silly and embarrassing.

Great actors but without knowledge of political science. Know nothing, virtue signaling, $$$ alliance.

Not true liberals, they are leftist fascists. Demand total agreement for a prescriptive list.

Once you have your psychic opening, gestalt switch or paradigm change it all looks stupid/deranged.

A healthy party would never be bulldozed by the Clinton Cartel.

THE END OF A BEND?

His wife died then he committed suicide. This also happens after divorce--men really love their wives.

Instead of learning reading, writing, arithmetic they learn how to freak out over certain words I think.

I don't care about your party ideas I just wanna know what is reasonable and true. Tucker Carlson

It's just common sense but there's been such a war on common sense for so long we got dense.

We can't live with injustice so of course we wanna see them get theirs.

I can't abide any thought other than my own. SJW worlview

Princess Diana was a national security threat, wielding a power far greater than they dared to allow.

We're promoting Magna Carta, Renaissance, 1776, what works: not the sleazy and sick from jerks.

In the land of the blind the one-eyed man is king. Erasmus

All my life I warned people, it turned out that I was right, and they hated me for it! Alex Jones

Giant monolithic corporations that control reality.

Pray McMaster outa the Whitehouse. In Jesus name he's gotta go, the louse.

No surprise: Google, twitter now ideological safe spaces where conservatives are

THE HERD IN WORDS
HIX POLITIX
HOW THEY RUINED US
JUST SKIP DINNER
LE FEMME AND THE COMMUNIST SPIRIT
LIBERAL CHAOS & ROT
LIBERAL DOUBLETHINK
LIBERAL GALL 1 & 2
LIBERAL SHOVE-DOWNS
LOCK YOUR GATE
MANUAL FOR SUPERIOR MEN
MODERN ART FROM HELL
MOSTLY FAKE
NOTES TO CHAMPS 1 & 2
OVERCOME FRENEMIES
PC MAKES US CRAZY
PEOPLE ARE CRUEL
PEOPLE PROBLEMS 1 & 2
PERSECUTED GENIUIS
POLI-PSYCH MYSTERIES
PRETENTIOUS SLOBS
QUEEN BEE
RETURNING TO FIRST NATURE
THE SCHOOLS SCREWED EM UP
SEASON OF TREASON
SEPARATE MEANS HOLY
SOCIAL HYPNOTISM
SOLITUDE SOLUTION
SUPERCILIOUS
TOAD TO PRINCE
TRIALS CYCLES
TRUMP VS. GROUP
TRUST IN TRASH
THE TRUTH ABOUT PEOPLE
UNDERHEANDEDLY CLEVER
WALK TALL WITHIN WALLS
WE'RE NOT ALL ONE
WINNERS SKIP DINNER
WORK OR SMERK

KAREN KELLOCK PH.D.

M.S. Political Science, San Diego State. Ph.D. in Psychology, University of California Irvine. Postdoctoral: UCI School of Medicine, Dept. of Psychiatry [NIMH Grants]. Developed the Debris Theory of Disease, a theory of system pathology in 120 books and 22 textbooks for the general public. The theory has a general formula: All disease is obstruction, all recovery is elimination, all success is attraction. The three obstructions are people, habit and food. Remove obstruction and snap to your goals, waiting in the wings.